Strange Dreams

Volume 4: Collected Stories
& Drawings of Brian Andreas

StoryPeople
Decorah

ISBN 0-9642660-3-2

The people in this book, if at one time real, are now entirely fictitious, having been subjected to a combination of a selective memory and a fertile imagination. Any resemblance to real people you might know, even if they are the author's relatives, is entirely coincidental, and is a reminder that you are imagining the incidents in this book as much as the author is.

StoryPeople
P.O. Box 64
Decorah, IA 52101
USA
319.382.8060
319.382.0263 FAX

storypeople@storypeople.com
http://www.storypeople.com/

First Edition: *September, 1996*
Second Printing: *February, 1998*

Printed at the West Coast Print Center, Berkeley, California

To my parents & grandparents, who gave me from an early age a world filled with wonder & possibility & love.

& to my sons, David Quinn & Matthew Shea, for the joy of melting ice cream cones & catching fireflies on warm summer nights & always, to Ellen, my friend & my love, with thanks for her grace & strength & willingness to follow wherever her heart sings.

Other books by Brian Andreas available
from StoryPeople Press:

Mostly True
Still Mostly True
Going Somewhere Soon

Cover Art: Brian Andreas
Back photo: Jon Duder

Strange Dreams

Introduction

In the three short years since I began, StoryPeople have gone from my small studio in Berkeley to the homes of collectors all over the world. The highest compliments still come in the form of letters, with many of you writing of how you found your story, how you **knew** it was yours. In those letters so many of you wonder where StoryPeople came from. I think it somehow appropriate to try & answer that question in this book, *Strange Dreams.*

Where did StoryPeople come from? Like pearls on a necklace, I can pick out important points that lead one into the next. I started out as a playwright, later abandoning theatre like everybody else who moves to L.A.. But that sense of a world filled with characters never left me, no matter how much the heat shimmered off the Hollywood Hills. After that, I carved marble, slowing down & listening to the stone tell me what it needed. In that slowing down, I learned the dialogue that is at the center of art & life. There are no clear & final answers, there are only discussions & thoughts & silent wonder filling each moment.

Those are some of the places StoryPeople came from. There are others, too. Ellen telling me we needed more color in our house. Raising children, laughing & yelling & wondering how to teach them about the world we each knew. The time constraint children bring with them; instead of weeks to complete a piece, now I had an hour a day. I started writing on restaurant napkins, in between mopping up spilled water & the ketchup-covered faces of the boys.

Those are all reasons, yet none of them are the **real** reasons for StoryPeople. I like to tweak people. I like to play. I like to laugh. I like to speak in accents of people from far-off, vaguely recognizable places. I like to walk in the mud & let the rain run down my back. I like to walk up slowly to cats & then bark so loud I scare them silly. I like to speak to the dead. I like to squish all of my family together in a big chair & watch videos & pick out the popcorn kernels with the most butter on them before Ellen gets to them. I like to dream up advertising promotions for new religions. I like to stare into the fire & listen to the shadows whisper their secrets. I like to stand up in public places & ask people why we can't do things another way. I like to act as if I know everything on certain days. On other days, I admit to knowing nothing. I like to remember that this is only one life & I'll probably look back at the end & say "O, that's what I was doing". I like to take time to listen to my heart, because it hasn't led me astray yet.

Where did StoryPeople come from? I have to admit I don't know. I like to think they were always here. I noticed them enough to remark on them, but they were here before me. They might have been here before all of us. Certainly, for me, it's hard to imagine a world without them.

In the end, I don't know if this helps you with the facts. I'm not very good with facts. I only know what's true...

With love,

Brian Andreas
17 September 1996

It was a strange
dream, she said

& I don't
remember a thing
except it kept
my attention the
whole time.

Strange Dream

The top of his head was
open up to the sky & when
he walked down the street
he'd end up with strange
things in there like the
number of dogs in China,
or the time it takes to
cook a pig.

It's not really useful,
he said, but I'd miss
this stuff if it ever
closed up.

Open to the Sky

he tried hard
to tell the truth
but it wasn't
always that
obvious, so
usually he
just said the first thing that
came to mind

First Thing

My sister read somewhere once that if you look into your own eyes long enough in a mirror you change into the Devil

LEiSURELY
threats

& it took her almost thirty years, but she finally did it.

Mirror Image

She said you know what
heaven is like? & I said
I wasn't sure & she laughed
& said grownups didn't
know much at all about
important, stuff & I said
I had to agree with her
even though I was one of
them myself.

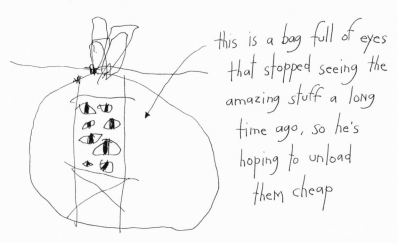

this is a bag full of eyes
that stopped seeing the
amazing stuff a long
time ago, so he's
hoping to unload
them cheap

Heaven

I used to hate
birthdays, she
told me, until
I figured out
I was the Queen
of the Universe

& now I do them
for the little
people.

Do you know all these people?
she whispered to me

& I
said, no, they're just here for the
free food & she said, But it's only
a dream & I said, I know. That's
why I can afford to do it.

Free Food

If I love you with
all my heart, she
said, what will you
give me?

    & then she stopped &
    said I didn't have to
    answer that because
    she was going to
    do it anyway.

when she held out
her arms, the
world
itself
wrapped
around
me & held
me tight

The World Itself

I remember we sat in the swing
on the front porch & as the dusk
came on us like a song, dark
throated & sweet, he told me
about the beginning when we
had bones of light & hair that
burned like the sun & I asked
what happened then?

& I felt him floating there in
the soft dark & finally he said
we forgot & I said I never would,
but sometimes I do & I understand
now why he put his arm around
me & said nothing more.

Bones of Light

this is a bag filled with dreams & recipes for Soup

& he's deciding right now which he's really hungry foR

Decisions

I have to buy all my presents at the last minute, she said,

or I get too excited & just give them away.

Last Minute

Even if I only need
this stuff once my
whole life, she said,
it's worth it

& besides, I paid
too much to get
rid of it yet.

My grandmother kept a box of
old photos in her attic & we used
to go up there on rainy days &
sit on the floor in the dusty light
& go through them & she would
tell about witches & broken
hearts & how we came from
royal blood & it was all there in
the pictures, she said

   & then we'd lose the light &
   we'd all go downstairs for
   dinner & in our secret hearts
   we sat taller knowing once
   we had ruled the world.

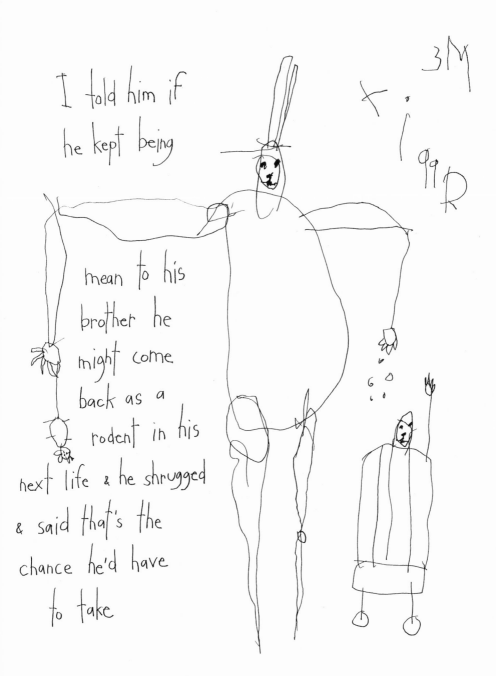

I told him if
he kept being

mean to his
brother he
might come
back as a
rodent in his
next life & he shrugged
& said that's the
chance he'd have
to take

I think you love
people until you
get to understand
them, she said

& I said, what
happens then?

& she said, o,
that's when you
move away.

Moving Day

I remember when the whales had wings, she said. Whatever happened? I said. It got to be too noisy with all the airplanes & other stuff, so they flew into the ocean & never came back. Some days, she added, I think about going, too.

Whales

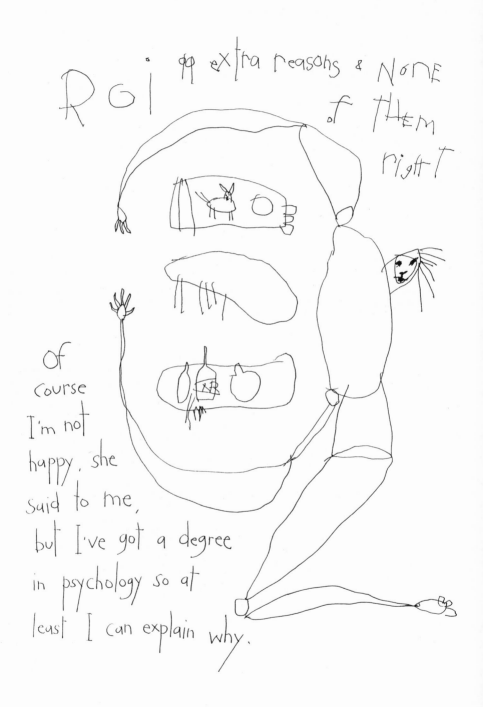

RoI 99 extra reasons & NONE of them right

Of course I'm not happy, she said to me, but I've got a degree in psychology so at least I can explain why.

Psychology

When I was young,
my grandma always
used to say it was
good I didn't get my
dad's nose & I thought
so, too,

but I always wondered
if someone somewhere
was walking around
without a nose because
of me.

I yell way too much at my kids, but they're smart enough

to read between the noise .

Between the Noise

Whenever she stood
in line at the bank
or while waiting
for the bus, I noticed
her feet.

The right always in
front & perpendicular
to the left just so.

Even after 2
children she
still dreamed
of being a
dancer.

Ballerina Mom

You have to
be blasé about
something,
she said,
otherwise
you'd die of
overexcitement.

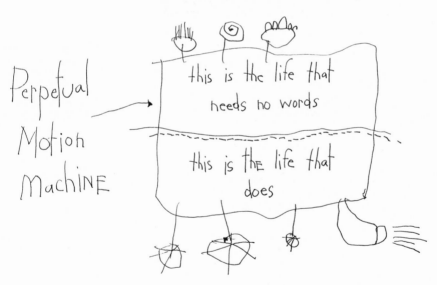

this is the moon dark
as a bird wing & softer,
he said & at that moment
I knew only the joy
of my child

My favorite time
of day is just at dark
when all thoughts of
what must get done
stop

& small pools of light
come alive on
tired faces
everywhere

Pools of Light

She asked me if I had kids & when I said I did she said make sure you teach them what's right & I said how will I know?

& she nodded & said. good point, just don't teach them any obvious wrong then.

Teaching Right

I didn't listen
to her because
she was my mother

& wouldn't
know anything
until I was
much older

Hindsight

I have to apologize beforehand
for anything
that happens,
he told her.

I haven't been dating that
long & my lizard brain still acts up sometimes.

Lizard Brain

He really
doesn't
have that
much to
say, she
told me,
so don't
get him
started.

It's lucky I only have
one of these, he said.

I can see where you'd never think about anything else.

Nothing to Say

My uncle Orbert had
only 3 fingers on his
left hand. He lost the
others during corn
planting one spring.

My fingers are buried
out in those fields
somewhere, he used to
tell us, & I check for
them every summer to
see if they've sprouted
yet.

cans of beans
& other small
things you throw
in jello when you've
lost the will to
go on

I asked him once
what he'd do if they
ever did sprout. He
thought for a minute.
I'd run like hell, he
said, & never look
back

& then he made us
promise not to tell
my aunt.

I don't care
what you do
when I'm gone,
he told us.
Just don't bury
me where the
dog can find
me.

These
knees have
stories,
she said,
but they'd
have to be
a mouth
to tell
you.

You don't
really notice
how much of
this stuff
has sharp edges
until it gets dark

Knees

I'm much better at the brotherhood of man thing, he said, when I can afford to live in a good neighborhood.

Brotherhood of Man

I learned 2 things early
on, my sister said.

The first is don't blame
people for being the
way they are.

What's the second? I said.

She smiled.

If they're really stupid,
she said, go ahead & blame
them.

It's a really simple
philosophy, she added.

I need someone
to invent a mirror
that leaves out
some of the details,
she said.

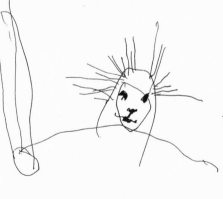

the real problem
with details
is there's
so many of
them

There's lots of stuff I want, she said, but I'm holding off until I get a bigger place.

I was greedier
when I was younger,
he said to me, because
I was stronger &
could lift more.

Greed

Sometimes you just
need the right
accessory, she said

& I said I know,
sometimes it takes
me an hour to pick
the right head

      & she just
      ignored me.

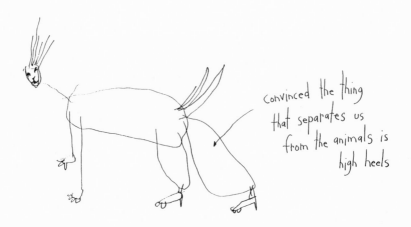

Convinced the thing
that separates us
from the animals is
high heels

Perfect Match

I don't wear
stuff to impress
people, she said.
I can't afford it yet.

secure in the
knowledge that
it's hard to
ruin mashed
potatoes

Cannibal

It's an invention, he said. What's it do? I said.

I don't know, he said. It's not finished yet.

Are you here
to borrow money
or to visit? he
used to say

& I'd say it's
me, grandpa

& then he'd say
o hell, come on
in & visit anyway.

I'm not worried about
ghosts in general, she said.
Just the ones that are
related to me.

Norm

We looked at the numbers on the blackboard & after awhile I finally asked if they made sense to him & he said no, I think they're just there to keep the riff-raff out.

Higher Math

He loved
her for
almost
everything
she
was

no good
with
figures

& she
decided
that was
enough
to let
him stay for a very long time.

Mr. Right

I only promise
the little things.

The big things don't
pay attention to what
I want anyhow.

Promises

this is the wind
what blows,
he said,

& it lives

in a jar in my bed

& his eyes were big
with the knowing
of all that

this is a box filled with
the sorrow of all the people
who have been forgotten

& some day it will
wash the world clean

The Wind What Blows

she turned to me &
whispered, don't you
just love it when you
get so excited you
forget to breathe?

& the thought of
her smiling eyes
still makes me
laugh.

over the years, she filled herself
with the best the world could offer,
but she still kept a little place
open for frozen peas

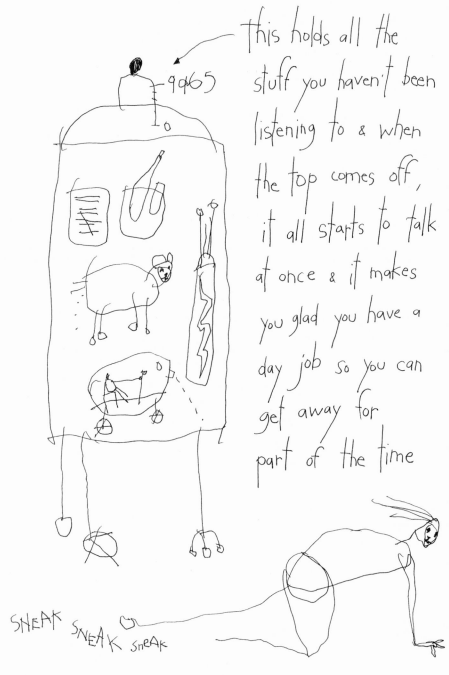

this holds all the
stuff you haven't been
listening to & when
the top comes off,
it all starts to talk
at once & it makes
you glad you have a
day job so you can
get away for
part of the time

SNEAK SNEAK SNEAK

Day Job

Once she told me she
was an ocean person
& when she combed
her fingers through
the seaweed she heard
the songs of the
mermaids & it was
easy to believe all
the old stories.

Mermaid Song

She held her grief behind her eyes
like an ocean

& when she leaned
forward into the
day it
spilled onto
the floor

& she
wiped at
it quickly
with her foot
& pretended no one had seen

Hidden Ocean

I have to hate
you, she said.

You know too
much about
me to be
trusted.

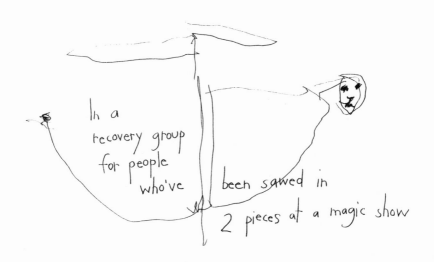

In a
recovery group
for people
who've been sawed in
2 pieces at a magic show

Know Too Much

I know I don't
go to church as
often as I should,
she said,

but I still
wear pantyhose
& that should
count for
something.

Rules that
make no
SENSE when
you stop to
think about it

Penance

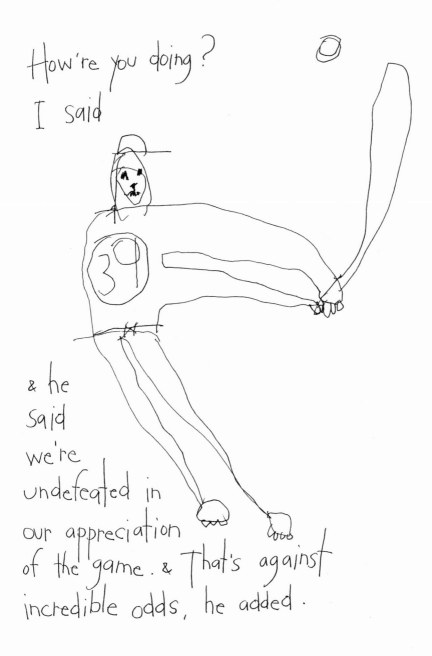

How're you doing?
I said

& he
said
we're
undefeated in
our appreciation
of the game. & That's against
incredible odds, he added.

Slow Pitch

If they'd listen to
me this world'd be
a better place, my
grandpa used to say

    &my grandma always
    nodded & said, You're
    right. Someday we're
    going to kick ourselves
    for that one & he'd frown
    & turn off his hearing aid.

Advice

I try not to cry about everything I've done wrong, she said, because I don't get enough fluids as it is already

Enough Fluid

She laid on
my chest &
her breathing
filled me
almost to beyond
what I could
hold

Almost Beyond

It's much easier
to trust the universe
when it's going
well, she said.

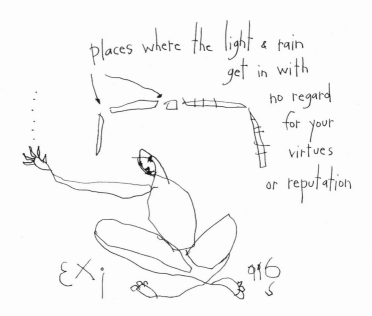

Trusting the Universe

My dad always
told me, The
right tool for
the right job,
but all he ever
had around were
a few screwdrivers,
so he ended up
using the telephone
a lot.

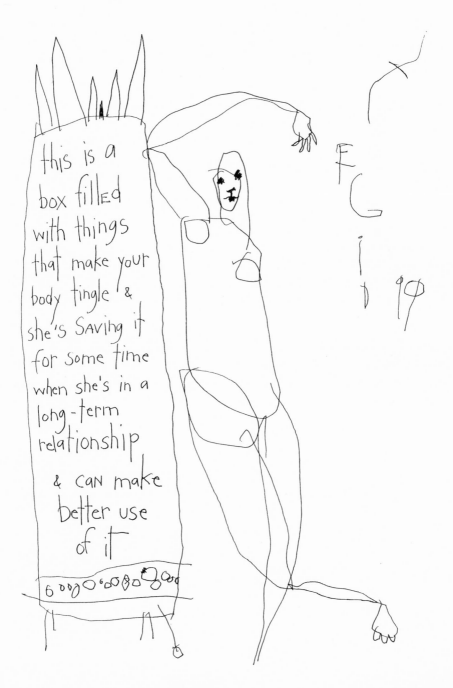

this is a box filled with things that make your body tingle & she's saving it for some time when she's in a long-term relationship & can make better use of it

Body Stuff

this is a sideways ladder because she likes to feel she's making progress.

but she's afraid of heights

fairly small but significant dance steps you can practice in the privacy of your own home

Sideways Ladder

I held her close
for only a short
time, but after
she was gone, I'd
see her smile on
the face of a
perfect stranger
& I knew she
would be there
with me all the
rest of my days.

I only hate
people that
deserve it,
she said.
How do you
know? I said.
Trust me, she
said. I know.

portable fires of
hell in case people
seem to be having too good a time

She kept a box of letters & dried flowers & some old chocolate in a dark place & watered it until it started to rot & then she put on her best dress

& some bright lipstick & took it around to everybody she knew & said, see, I told you so.

Expectation

If this ever gets off the ground, he said, it'll probably be really dangerous & maybe I'll finally get the respect I deserve

He sneaked through the world like night itself

& never gave himself a chance to love.

Night Itself

Ruler of the Universe

we grow a
lot faster
than trees,
he said, so
we miss a
lot of stuff

Growing Fast

hasn't started to
make sense
of the world yet

but
thinks
it's
beautiful
all the same

PLANTer of
things that
dry out
when you
don't water
them ever

Making Sense

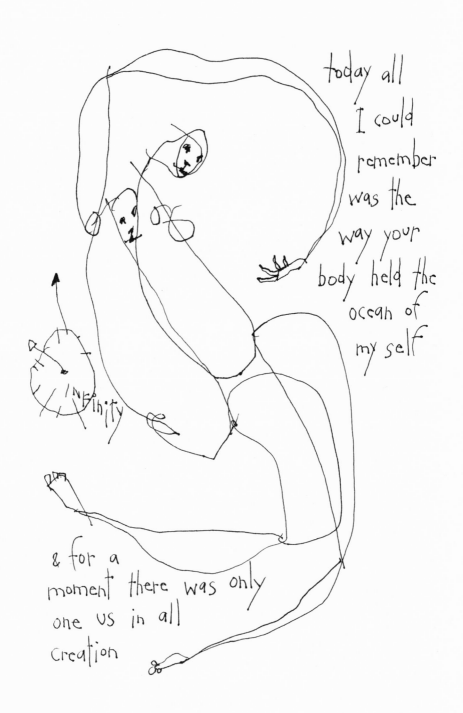

today all
I could
remember
was the
way your
body held the
ocean of
my self

INFINITY

& for a
moment there was only
one us in all
creation

One Us

When I was younger, my
favorite thing was riding
the pony outside the Safeway.
My dad always said I should
save my money for something
better, but I could ride
for miles all over the West
& always end up back at the
Safeway

        & all it cost was a
        quarter & I still can't
        think of anything
        better than that.

Riding the Pony

Anybody can make
up past lives,
she said.

The real
trick is to
make up future lives
& not forget you did it.

Future Lives

All this stuff
will make perfect
sense later on,
he used to say,
if you can
remember
enough of it.

About the Artist

Brian Andreas is a fiber artist, sculptor, and storyteller. He uses traditional media from fine art, theatre and storytelling, as well as computer networks and multimedia to explore new forms of human community. He also likes to put things together with the rustiest stuff he can find. His work is shown and collected internationally.

Born in 1956 in Iowa City, Iowa, he holds a B.A. from Luther College in Decorah, Iowa, and an M.F.A. in Fiber and Mixed Media from John F. Kennedy University in Orinda, California.

After years of adventure on the West Coast of the United States, he now lives together with Ellen Rockne, and their two wild and beautiful boys in northeast Iowa among the Lutherans. He still writes on restaurant napkins, and reminisces about great meals he's had in other places.

About StoryPeople

StoryPeople are wood sculptures, three to four feet tall, in a roughly human form. They can be as varied as a simple cutout figure, or an assemblage of found and scrap wood, or an intricate, roughly made treasure box. Each piece uses only recycled barn and fence wood from old homesteads in the northeast Iowa area. Adding to their individual quirkiness are scraps of old barn tin and twists of wire. They are painted with bright colors and hand-stamped, a letter at a time, with original stories. The most striking aspect of StoryPeople are the shaded spirit faces. These faces are softly blended into the wood surface, and make each StoryPerson come alive.

Every figure is signed and numbered by the artist. The stories are used for a limited number of times, and each figure is unique because of the materials used. The figures, the colorful story prints, and the books, are available in galleries and stores throughout the US and Canada. Please feel free to call or write for more information.

StoryPeople
P.O. Box 64
Decorah, IA 52101
USA

319.382.8060
319.382.0263 FAX

storypeople@storypeople.com
http://www.storypeople.com